# FORENSIC SCIENCE

## Alex Frith

Designed by Stephen Moncrieff
Illustrated by Kuo Kang Chen,
Lee Montgomery and Stephen Moncrieff
Comic strips illustrated by Sherwin Schwartzrock

Consultant: Peter White, Professor of Forensic Science,
University of Lincoln

Devised by Georgina Andrews
Edited by Jane Chisholm
Series designer: Mary Cartwright

# Contents

Page 4-5    **Who's who** in the world of crime and detection.

CHAPTER 1:  **Science and law**
Page 6-13   Find out what 'forensic science' really means. Look over a crime scene and into a trial to see how scientists can help.

CHAPTER 2:  **Written in sweat**
Page 14-20  Examine a fingerprint up close to see its identifying features. Learn how experts find suspicious prints at a crime scene.

CHAPTER 3:  **Written in blood**
Page 21-27  Look at the patterns of blood at the scene of a burglary, and find out what tests scientists can do to examine blood stains.

CHAPTER 4:  **Secrets in the cells**
Page 28-35  Find out how the discovery of DNA revolutionized detective work, and how scientists use DNA evidence to solve crimes.

CHAPTER 5:  **The talking dead**
Page 36-43  Examine a body to find out how marks left on it after death can show when a person died, and what killed them.

CHAPTER 6:  **Clues from nature**

Page 44-51  Find out how scientists can find all sorts of useful clues about crimes from insects, animals, plants and even soil.

CHAPTER 7:  **The little things**

Page 52-59  Search a crime scene in the woods for tiny traces left behind, and find out how microscopes can reveal vital clues.

CHAPTER 8:  **Going ballistic**

Page 60-67  Learn how a gun works, and explore the aftermath of a gun battle to see what evidence is left behind.

CHAPTER 9:  **Exploding evidence**

Page 68-74  Find out how bombs work and fires start. Then learn what scientists can do to prove who was responsible.

CHAPTER 10:  **The paper trail**

Page 75-81  Examine suspicious handwriting to see if it is genuine, and find out what clues can be found on computer drives.

CHAPTER 11:  **Criminal identity**

Page 82-89  Find out how criminals can give themselves away by their face, voice and even the way they behave.

Page 90-91  **Timeline of forensic science**

Page 92-93  **Glossary**

Page 94  **Internet links**

Page 95  **Index**

Page 96  **Acknowledgements**

# Who's who

Many people are involved in criminal investigations. Different names are given to people who are affected by a crime, and all the different people who help to solve it. This section explains who they all are, what they do – and it shows how scientists get involved.

## Victim

All crimes end up hurting someone. That person is described as the victim, whether the crime is a simple theft or a horrendous murder.

## Suspect

If the police have a good idea about who committed the crime, that person is called a suspect. Suspects can be arrested and kept in prison for a short time, but they must be treated as if they are innocent until they are proven guilty.

## Witness

Anyone who saw or heard something happening that relates to a crime is a witness. They can help the police to work out what happened. Sometimes witnesses can become suspects, especially if they are found to be lying.

## Crime scene investigator

Also known as CSIs, these people have the job of checking the scene of a crime for evidence. They take photos and collect samples to send to labs for testing. They do not have to be police officers or scientists, but they can be both.

## Police officer

Police officers are in charge of solving a crime. Senior officers called detectives piece together all the evidence. Junior officers guard crime scenes, track down witnesses and arrest suspects for the detectives to interview.

## Forensic scientist

Any scientist who helps the police or a lawyer by examining and testing evidence is doing forensic science work. Some scientists specialize in this kind of work, and are based in crime labs – these are dedicated forensic scientists.

After a suspect is arrested, he or she is put on trial for their crime. Forensic scientists can play an important part here, too. Lots of other people get involved in a trial as well. In some countries, different types of people do some of these jobs.

## Defendant

The defendant is the person accused of the crime. In some courts they have a special place to stand called a dock. In others, they sit at a table with their lawyer.

## Lawyer

In court, lawyers present evidence to prove that a defendant did or did not commit a crime. In most countries, one team of lawyers – the 'prosecution' team – tries to prove the defendant's guilt. The defendant has a team who argues against them.

## Coroner

When a person dies and no one is sure why, a coroner may be called in. He or she works with doctors, lawyers and witnesses in a special trial called an inquest. The coroner decides how a person died, and whether or not it was suspicious.

## Expert witness

An expert 'witness' is not someone who saw the crime happening. Instead, it's a scientist or expert who has examined a vital clue to a case. In court, expert witnesses explain to the judge and jury what they discovered, and what this means.

## Judge

A judge is the person in charge of the trial. He or she has the power to decide whether or not any evidence presented is solid enough to be used. In some trials, judges also decide on a defendant's guilt or innocence.

## Jury

Many trials are presented to a jury of people who do not know anything about the crime. It's their job to listen to the evidence presented by lawyers and witnesses, to weigh all the arguments, and then to decide if the defendant is guilty or not.

CHAPTER 1

CHAPTER **1**
# Science and law

**T**he word 'forensic' means *to do with the law*. So forensic *science* means using scientific knowledge and techniques to help with a criminal investigation, especially in a trial. But most people use it to mean *science that solves crimes*.

Every day, forensic scientists are hard at work in dedicated crime labs. They use tests to analyze evidence from crime scenes. If the tests they use reveal anything useful about a criminal case, the same scientists are often also called upon to be expert witnesses in a trial. They will explain what the test results mean. This can make all the difference in proving whether a person is guilty or innocent.

## Pieces of you

Stop reading for a second, and take a look down at the floor. Can you see anything there? If you were able to look really closely, you would find little pieces of yourself. Minuscule fragments of your skin, hair and clothes fall off all the time without you noticing. If you know what to look for, you'll see all types of telltale signs that link directly to you, and you only. However hard you might try not to, you leave a unique trace wherever you go.

Now take a good look at yourself. Look under your fingernails, and on the soles of your shoes. Check your pockets, and sniff your clothes. Tiny strands from a carpet might be stuck to you. Some smells from the air might be sticking to your hair and clothes.

Everywhere you go, you always leave some traces of yourself behind, and in turn you always pick up some traces of the places you've been to – and of the people you've brushed against. Normally these traces are not at all interesting, but when a crime is committed, they become vital clues. These tiny traces may be able to tell who committed the crime, when and even how.

**FORENSIC FACT**

Everyday objects are full of clues that can be linked to a specific person. Some of them have more obvious clues than others.

Telephones show you the last numbers called.

Cards in a wallet can reveal the identity of the owner.

Dirt and litter stuck to a shoe show where a person has just been.

The owner of this piece of litter might have drink stains on their clothes.

A CSI collects a sample of blood from a crime scene using a cotton swab.

## Making evidence talk

Almost anything found at a crime scene might turn out to be evidence that helps to solve the crime – from something as obvious as a blood stain to something as innocent as a piece of carpet fluff. Specially trained Crime Scene Investigators (CSIs) collect this evidence and then pass it on to the police detective in charge of the investigation. It's the detective's job to sort through the evidence. Some of it will need to be tested, and the detective passes each item of evidence along to the right forensic science team, and asks them what to analyze.

Clues such as fingerprints and bullets are so common to police work that there are specialized crime labs to test these things in many large police stations. But some crimes are solved by much more unusual clues, such as animal hair or flecks of paint. Then, detectives contact a relevant scientific specialist to help.

Sadly, so many crimes are committed every day that the police and the scientists who help them can't investigate everything. So a lot of forensic work is reserved only for serious crimes, such as terrorist bombings, industrial pollution, and gruesome murder...

# The acid bath murderer

**Place:** London, UK

**Date:** 1951

**Crime:** serial murder

**Latest victim:** Olive Durand-Deacon

**Chief suspect:** John Haigh, salesman

**Incriminating evidence:** Haigh was the last person to see Olive alive, and was caught trying to sell some of her furs and pearls.

**Suspect's statement:** "Yes, I killed her! And eight others before that! But you'll never prove it in court, because I destroyed the bodies with deadly acid! Hah!"

**Forensic breakthrough:** at Haigh's warehouse, the police found a pile of acid sludge on the floor. Scientist Keith Simpson poked through the pile carefully, and managed to find a gallstone and a handful of false teeth that had resisted the acid. He used dental records in court to prove that they belonged to Mrs. Durand-Deacon.

**Verdict:** guilty

**Sentence:** death

Haigh filled an old bathtub full of acid and left his victims in it until their bodies dissolved.

## Science at the crime scene

Forensic work usually begins when the police are called to the scene of a crime. A CSI team will seal off the scene. They have to decide which evidence will be useful to detectives and scientists, and then make sure it is properly collected. Police detectives will decide which samples to send to different forensic science labs to be analyzed. Sometimes, a scientist will be called in to examine something big or urgent at the scene, but this is rare.

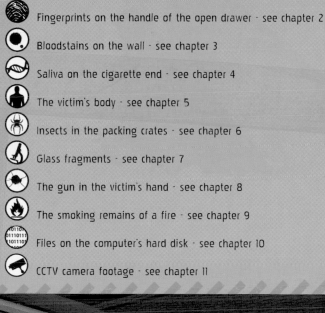

# Crime scene: city import office

There are many different types of evidence at this scene for CSIs to collect and for scientists to examine.

Fingerprints on the handle of the open drawer · see chapter 2

Bloodstains on the wall · see chapter 3

Saliva on the cigarette end · see chapter 4

The victim's body · see chapter 5

Insects in the packing crates · see chapter 6

Glass fragments · see chapter 7

The gun in the victim's hand · see chapter 8

The smoking remains of a fire · see chapter 9

Files on the computer's hard disk · see chapter 10

CCTV camera footage · see chapter 11

## Science in the courtroom

In a trial, expert witnesses have to be cross-examined by the defendant's lawyer. He or she will try to show either that the expert is not to be trusted, or that the tests they used were faulty. The case in this comic strip is fictional, but the problem described is all too real...

# CHAPTER 2

# Written in sweat

Y ou can't always see it, but whenever you touch something, your skin leaves behind a faint mark of sweat and grease. These marks have a pattern which matches the tiny network of ridges on the tips of your fingers. These ridges are usually called fingerprints, but you have them on your palms and feet, too.

Everybody's ridge patterns are slightly different – even identical twins have different ones – so anything you've touched can be linked directly to you and only you.

The first person to make use of fingerprints was a magistrate in India in the 19th century. When pensioners came to him each month to collect their pensions, he checked their identities using fingerprint record cards that he'd made.

By the early 20th century, police forces around the world had realized how useful fingerprints could be. They began to take ink fingerprints of every suspect arrested, so that they could compare them with prints found at crime scenes.

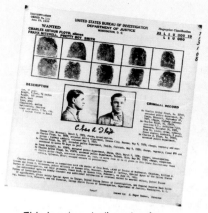

This is a 'wanted' poster for American gangster Pretty Boy Floyd. Police were asked to identify him using his fingerprints. These had been taken when he was arrested a few years earlier.

## Making a match

Nowadays, specialist fingerprint officers find and analyze suspicious prints at crime scenes. They can quickly compare these with prints taken from suspects. If they find at least six matching points shared by two prints, it means they both come from the same finger or thumb.

If you look closely at the ridges on a finger, you can see places where they split or come to an end, a little like in a maze.

Loop

Join

This is a print made of the same finger using ink. Computer programs can accurately compare two prints to see if the ridges join or split in the same places.

This chest of drawers has been burgled. A fingerprint officer will dust it for prints.

It's not usually hard to find clues at a crime scene. Fingerprints in particular tend to be found in obvious places. Look at the chest of drawers below. The first place to check would be the handles, and any objects that might have been moved, such as the mug on the top.

Fingerprint officers do have to be careful not to smudge any prints, though, and they take fingerprints from everyone who uses the chest. Most prints found on an object belong to the people who use it a lot - so these prints can be ignored. Then, any prints that don't match these people can be regarded as suspicious.

Fingerprints at crime scenes often show up clearly in thick dust, or in a smear of blood. These prints can be photographed. The photos are loaded into a computer, where they will be analyzed by a fingerprint expert.

Some prints are found by dusting an area using a silver or black powder. The powder sticks to the sweat, and reveals the unique print pattern. These kinds of prints are described as "latent" prints. The sweat that fingers leave

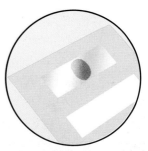

Powder is applied with a brush. It only sticks to the sweaty prints.

The powder showing the print mark is 'lifted' using a piece of sticky tape.

The tape is stuck to a plastic sheet, and the location is noted down.

behind is usually invisible to the naked eye, but it's still there.

As well as finding prints, fingerprint officers have to record exactly where they were found. This evidence can prove that a particular person touched something at a crime scene. Without this information, prints are useless in a trial.

## Chemicals and lights

Powder won't reveal all latent prints, because there are some surfaces that powder won't stick to – such as human skin. But scientists are always finding new ways to reveal the invisible marks left behind in sweat. Just wiping away a fingerprint is no longer enough to protect a criminal; only strong bleach can remove a print mark entirely.

A variety of chemical sprays can be applied to different surfaces to reveal latent prints. Cyanoacrylate is a substance used in superglue. As well as being sticky, it also reacts with human sweat and makes it white. Another chemical called ninhydrin reacts with human sweat in a different way – it turns purple.

These chemicals are useful on different surfaces. Ninhydrin can be used on wallpaper, and cyanoacrylate can be used to show up fingerprints on human skin. Normally, both sprays are used with a special torch that shines ultraviolet (UV) light. This makes it easier to see the patterns in latent prints.

Before he leaves, this criminal wipes the light switch with a cloth to remove his prints.

Later, a fingerprint officer sprays the area with ninhydrin.

The print on the switch is smudged and useless, but the spray has picked up latent prints on the walls.

# Roscoe's fingers

Some criminals wear gloves to avoid leaving fingerprints. But many others don't plan ahead. In the USA in 1941, one habitual thief thought of a way to be sure his fingerprints would never be found again. He would remove them...

MEET ROSCOE PHILLIPS, CAREER CRIMINAL...

EVERY TIME I GET ARRESTED, THE COPS KNOW I'M GUILTY 'COS OF MY STUPID FINGERS.

I NEED TO FIND A SURGEON...

YOU WANT ME TO REMOVE YOUR FINGERPRINTS? IMPOSSIBLE!

DR. P BRANDENBURG SURGEON

FIRST, I WILL SLICE THE SKIN FROM YOUR FINGERTIPS. THIS WILL HURT.

I CAN PAY YOU HANDSOMELY.

WELL, THERE IS ONE IDEA I HAVE...

AAAAAAARGH!

**FORENSIC FACT**

The Federal Bureau of Investigation (FBI) is the central crime-fighting force for the entire United States. It has a collection of over 50 million individual prints, all belonging to people convicted of a crime.

Databases like this can fail if a person's print was recorded badly, or if a person's fingerprints change, for example if they have an accident that leaves scars.

Fingerprints are still the single most common piece of evidence that convince a judge and jury to find someone guilty.

# Fingerprints on file

You can't tell anything about a person just from their fingerprints. All you can do is to see if they match any suspicious prints. But what if there is no suspect? Then detectives must turn to their records of fingerprints collected from criminals in the past.

Most countries keep a huge database with the fingerprints of anyone who has ever been convicted of a crime. So, whenever a suspicious print is found at an important crime scene, fingerprint officers can check to see if it matches a print in their database. Some people argue that everyone should register their fingerprints, so that the database has no gaps. But other people think this is a bad idea, because if anything goes wrong with it, innocent people could be arrested. What do you think?

In some countries, people carry identity cards with them. These cards have a record of a person's fingerprint on them, so it's impossible to use someone else's card.

Many identity cards show photos of the person they identify. Photos are much easier to forge than fingerprints.

Serial numbers make it harder for people to make fake cards.

An electronic version of the fingerprint is stored on the gold chip.

Other unique markings can be held on ID cards, such as a scan of your eye.

00 19749 3940 0224
Mr.I.D.Card

# CHAPTER 3

# Written in blood

Pumping around inside a typical human, there are at least 9 pints (5 l.) of thick, red, sticky blood. And, as you'll know if you've ever had a nosebleed or cut your finger, blood gets everywhere – and it leaves stains.

After a murder or a violent attack, there will often be bloodstains at the crime scene. Blood can reveal all kinds of vital clues about a fight. An expert in blood spatter patterns can tell how many people were involved, what weapons they used, and what order things happened in.

Detectives call on experts to examine the patterns that bloodstains are found in. They also send samples to serologists – scientists who study blood and other body fluids.

Because blood makes such a big mess, it's surprisingly common to find really obvious clues in it, like this mark left on the floor by a missing weapon.

## Forensic serology

If enough clean blood is found, serologists can run tests on it. They can try to identify how many different people's blood is at a scene, and then work out which bloodstains came from which person. This can help to prove who started the fight, and who held which weapon.

The first forensic blood tests were invented in the early 20th century. German Paul Uhlenhuth found a way to prove that a stain was actually blood. And Austrian Karl Landsteiner discovered that human blood comes in four main types – A, B, AB and O – as well as many subtypes. A simple lab process called electrophoresis can tell which type a sample of blood belongs to. This can prove that blood did *not* belong to someone, which is vitally important as it can quickly clear up a false arrest.

Drops of blood from one big sample can be treated with an 'anti-agent' to test for a person's blood group.

Blood from Type A

Blood from Type B

Blood reacts with different anti-agents depending on whether it is type A, B, AB or O.

# The carpenter's apron

**Place:** Gohren, Germany

**Date:** 1901

**Crime:** double murder

**Latest victims:** Peter and Hermann Stubbe

**Chief suspect:** Ludwig Tessnow, carpenter

**Previous history:** Tessnow had been accused of murdering two girls, and of slaughtering a local farmer's sheep. But there was no solid evidence to convict him of these crimes.

**Incriminating evidence:** Tessnow's apron was found, covered in red-brown stains.

**Suspect's statement:** "Of course there are lots of stains on my apron. They are wood dye. I am a hard-working carpenter, and I have many cans of dye in my workshop. Now leave me alone."

**Forensic breakthrough:** the local magistrate had read about Paul Uhlenhuth's new test. He sent across the apron, and Uhlenhuth found many wood dye stains – but also 17 human blood stains, and 9 sheep blood stains.

**Verdict:** guilty

**Sentence:** death

Tessnow committed his vile crimes with a hatchet. Nowadays, the blade could be tested for latent bloodstains.

## Patterns in blood

Some forensic scientists are experts in blood spatter patterns. They look at the way blood spreads out on the wall or floor to guess what kind of weapon was used, where the victim was standing, and how many times they were hit. Experts can usually tell the difference between blood from a bullet wound, a knife or a baseball bat.

Some blood spatter patterns can be caused by several different weapons, and patterns will look different if the blood hits a smooth surface such as glass, or a rough surface such as a carpet. Experts will match up the blood patterns with the other evidence found as best they can.

A thin streak means the blood came from an angle. The tail points in the direction the blood was moving.

### BLOOD FACT

Blood pumps away from a person's heart quickly through arteries. It goes back into the heart slowly through veins. So if an artery gets cut, lots of blood can spurt out, and it can spray really far. If a vein gets cut, blood will drip out of the body fairly slowly. Some blood spatters at crime scenes aren't from cuts, though. They come from blood that flies off the end of a weapon.

Thick spatters show that a large amount of blood came out all at once.

A spray of tiny spatters means that blood hit the wall really hard, perhaps after a hit with a heavy bat or even a bullet.

A roundish spatter happens when blood drips straight down onto a smooth surface, for example after a simple cut.

## The missing masterpiece

Below you can see a fictional crime scene with blood spatters all over it. In this type of situation, a police detective will ask a blood spatter expert and a serologist to help him or her work out what happened.

These two kinds of forensic scientists do an important job, but it's the detective who has to put all the pieces together. He or she will inspect the crime scene and talk to any witnesses, as well as checking any test results that the scientists provide. Seeing how all these pieces fit together might help to solve the crime.

Samples of blood from this crime scene would be carefully put into bags and sent to a serology lab to be examined.

### THEFT FACT

Thieves often cut paintings out of their frames to make it easier to carry them away.

Art dealers should be able to recognize when the edges of a famous painting are missing. This information can be used in court to prove that a painting was stolen.

### Crime scene: art gallery

The police were called in by a cleaner, who says that a thief stabbed him and stole a painting.

In reality, police would examine more clues than just the blood, but in this case the blood tells quite a tale on its own.

## The cleaner's statement

"It was crazy. I was mopping the floor when this guy came out of nowhere with a knife. I managed to smack him with my broom, but then he charged at me and stabbed me in the side. I pretended I was unconscious, and then I watched him cut out that painting. After he left I crawled to the phone and called for help."

### BLOOD FACT

Just like fingerprints, blood is very difficult to clean away. So even if it can't be seen, there might still be blood at a crime scene.

CSIs use chemical sprays and UV lights to search for blood, just like looking for latent prints.

This photo shows a latent boot print that showed up after being sprayed with luminol.

## Case closed

In the hospital, the detective has just listened to the cleaner's story. But it doesn't match up with the patterns of blood found at the crime scene. Perhaps the cleaner can't remember what happened very clearly – or perhaps he's lying.

One part of his story has been confirmed by the serologist, though: there were two people at the scene. The blood on the floor all seems to come from the cleaner (it has been matched with his blood type), but the blood spatters around the painting and on the broomstick have a different blood type. So, two people were at the scene, and two people were injured – but did they really get into a fight?

The detective believes that the cleaner and the thief may be friends. The cleaner let the thief in through a side door, then they hit each other to make it look as if a fight happened.

Take another look at the crime scene, and see what the detective thinks happened. Perhaps the cleaner will change his story...

The broom has blood on one end. It's likely that the cleaner really did attack the intruder with it.

The blood by the phone is the cleaner's. But the shoeprints belong to somebody else. The intruder must have left *after* the cleaner reached the phone.

There are bloodstains on the wall underneath where the painting used to be. So the cleaner must have hit him *after* the intruder had already cut the painting out.

Arresting the cleaner is one thing, but the police still need to find the thief and prove that he was involved. The next chapter explains how a serologist can do this, thanks to a chemical known as DNA, which can be found in blood.

If there was a fight, it's surprising that there isn't more blood and damage at this crime scene. Perhaps the cleaner let the intruder stab him to make his story more convincing.

**4**

# Secrets in the cells

**A**ll too many crime scenes are covered in blood, whether it belongs to one victim, many victims, or even the criminal who did it. Serologists have been able to find out some information about blood for over a hundred years, but a major breakthrough happened in 1955, when scientists discovered DNA. Now, serologsts can connect a bloodstain directly to the particular person the blood came from.

Di-oxy-ribo-Nu-cle-ic Acid, to use its full name, is the chemical that controls how our bodies are built. It does this by controlling the cells in our body. These are the building blocks that people are made of. DNA itself is an incredibly complicated chemical, made up of billions of parts known as genes. Genes help to control different things, such as the length of your toes or the size of your memory.

This is a cluster of skin cells.

Inside most cells is a nucleus. This tells the cell what to do.

Cell nucleus

Inside each nucleus is a long, twisted molecule of DNA.

## It has to be you

You inherit all your DNA from your parents. Exactly half the genes in your DNA come from your mother, and half from your father. There are so many ways in which these two halves can combine that it's impossible even for your brother or sister to have exactly the same code even as a coincidence. Only identical twins or clones share the same DNA.

Most bloodstains contain the DNA of the person they came from. But detectives had to wait a few years before they could use this information. In 1985, British scientist Alec Jeffreys worked out a way to extract and compare DNA from two separate samples. Using this technique, serologists compare DNA from a crime scene with DNA from a suspect. This process is often described as genetic fingerprinting. It's one of the most common tests in forensic science.

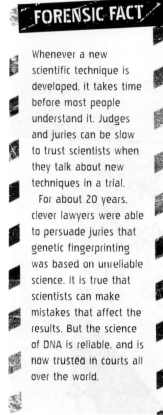

### FORENSIC FACT

Whenever a new scientific technique is developed, it takes time before most people understand it. Judges and juries can be slow to trust scientists when they talk about new techniques in a trial.

For about 20 years, clever lawyers were able to persuade juries that genetic fingerprinting was based on unreliable science. It is true that scientists can make mistakes that affect the results. But the science of DNA is reliable, and is now trusted in courts all over the world.

# The great DNA manhunt

Enderby, UK, 1987. The police were after a man who had murdered two women. The first ever forensic DNA test quickly proved that the chief suspect was innocent. And so a new kind of manhunt began...

IN LOCAL NEWS, POLICE ARE STILL HUNTING FOR THE ENDERBY KILLER. ALL MEN AGED 16-34 ARE REQUIRED TO GIVE A BLOOD SAMPLE.

THEY CAN'T DO THIS!

WHY'S THAT, COLIN?

I'VE GOT A CRIMINAL RECORD. IF I GIVE BLOOD, I'M BOUND TO GET INTO TROUBLE.

LOOK, IAN... I'LL PAY YOU £100 IF YOU PRETEND TO BE ME.

ALRIGHT. I'M NOT FROM ROUND HERE, ANYWAY.

A FEW WEEKS LATER, IAN WAS GETTING DRUNK WITH FRIENDS IN A LOCAL PUB.

KING'S HEAD

MY MATE COLIN, HE'S A REAL WEIRDO.

OH YEAH?

YOU REMEMBER THAT DNA THING UP IN ENDERBY? COLIN PAID ME £100 TO GIVE MY BLOOD INSTEAD OF HIS.

REALLY? YOU KNOW, THEY NEVER DID FIND THE KILLER.

I'D BETTER TELL THE POLICE ABOUT THIS!

THE POLICE RUSHED TO THE BAKERY WHERE COLIN WORKED AND ARRESTED HIM.

HE AGREED TO GIVE THEM A SAMPLE OF HIS BLOOD THIS TIME. SURE ENOUGH, HIS DNA MATCHED WITH SAMPLES ON BOTH VICTIMS. COLIN PITCHFORK IS STILL IN PRISON TODAY.

RATS! CAUGHT OUT BY MY OWN BODY.

## DNA profile

Since 1985, scientists have developed many new ways to process a DNA sample. They all require special equipment and chemicals, but the specific method used depends on how large the sample is. One of the most common methods is known as Short Tandem Repeat (STR) analysis. In this process, the serologist chemically highlights 13 sections of human DNA. These 13 sections are then printed onto a sheet called a profile. Samples of DNA that have been taken from several different places can be printed onto the same profile, so it's easy to see if they match.

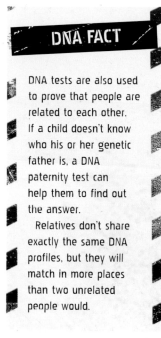

### DNA FACT

DNA tests are also used to prove that people are related to each other. If a child doesn't know who his or her genetic father is, a DNA paternity test can help them to find out the answer.

Relatives don't share exactly the same DNA profiles, but they will match in more places than two unrelated people would.

Each person's profile spreads down the page, a little like a long bar code.

The lines on the profile vary in thickness depending on a person's genes.

CRIME SCENE SAMPLE

SUSPECT 1

SUSPECT 2

SUSPECT 3

SUSPECT 4

The first profile shows the crime scene sample. The rest show samples taken from a number of different suspects.

Suspect 4 has a profile that matches the evidence profile very closely. And all the other suspects can be ruled out.

## Finding DNA

One reason why DNA can be found at many crime scenes is because criminals don't know how to clean it up. DNA can be found in all types of things, and is often too small to see without looking very closely.

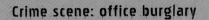

### Crime scene: office burglary

CSIs found no fingerprints in the room, but there are all sorts of places to check for DNA. Where would you look?

- Any objects that have definitely had human contact: saliva on the apple core, skin cells on the ring, hair on the hairbrush.

- Anything that is out of place: knocked-over chair, plant pot, sweat marks on the pieces of paper. All of these might have flakes of hair and skin from the burglar.

DNA can be found in so many things that it can seem as if every crime scene is littered with the stuff. This in itself can be a major problem for detectives. DNA evidence is amazingly useful, but only if it's big enough or clean enough for a scientist to use.

## DNA difficulties

Crimes that take place on the street, or in a busy building, can be very awkward for the police when they are looking for clues. There will be a lot of DNA in the area because of all the people who walk through it every day. Even if there is something obvious, like a pool of blood, it could be contaminated with DNA from other people's skin or hair that may have fallen into it.

Another sad problem is that there is so much DNA evidence from crime scenes that serology labs often have huge piles of evidence to examine, much of which will turn out to be useless.

It's not all bad news for detectives, though. DNA can remain at a crime scene for years. Even bones that are thousands of years old still contain DNA that can be extracted and tested. Scientists are improving analysis techniques all the time, and DNA may soon overtake fingerprints as the most common evidence used in solving crimes.

**CSI FACT**

When gathering evidence from a murder scene, CSIs need to wear protective coveralls. This is to make sure that they don't drop any of their own DNA onto the scene.

Samples of human body tissue must be carefully collected and tagged. Different types of bags, jars and tubes are used to keep the evidence safe.

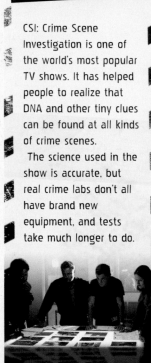

## DNA on trial

Once a suspect has been accused of a crime, any DNA samples that link that person to the scene of the crime, or to the victim, or a murder weapon, can be very compelling to a judge and jury. Many people on juries already know a little about DNA evidence, and they understand that it is unique to a person.

In fact, DNA has become so well-known that some juries expect it to feature in any trial, especially a murder. This is sometimes called the 'CSI' effect, named after the long-running TV series about a forensic science team.

But DNA evidence is not always relevant. For example, DNA found on a murder weapon can prove that a particular person touched it, but it can't prove how the DNA got there. As with all branches of forensics, DNA evidence usually needs to be combined with witness testimony to paint a full picture of what happened. Just sometimes, though, DNA is a crucial witness...

# An innocent man

**Place:** Baltimore, USA

**Date:** 1983

**Crime:** murder

**Victim:** Dawn Hamilton

**Chief suspect:** Kirk Bloodsworth, ex-marine

**Incriminating evidence: 1.** Eyewitness report of a man seen running away from the scene matches Kirk's description.
**2.** Kirk was reported by friends as acting strange that day.

**Suspect's statement:** "I'd just had an argument with my wife. That's why I was acting funny. I never saw the girl."

**Verdict:** guilty

**Forensic breakthrough:** DNA testing didn't exist in 1983, but 10 years later, stains on the victim's clothing were finally sent for DNA analysis.

**New verdict:** this DNA did not match Kirk Bloodsworth's – and he was finally released.

**Case closed:** in 2003, the real killer was found using a DNA database search: K. S. Ruffner. His DNA was on file because he was in prison for another crime.

Samples of Kirk's DNA and the crime scene DNA were sent to two different labs for double-checking.

# 5

# The talking dead

**M**urder investigations often begin with a dead body. If you know how to examine it and what to look for, a body can tell you a lot about what happened, even though it can't talk.

Who is it? When did they die? How did they die? These are the key questions for a detective hoping to catch and convict the killer. The 'who' is often the trickiest part, but finding out how and when a person died is usually a straightforward matter for a doctor who specializes in death, known as a pathologist.

# Time of death

Knowing the exact moment when a person died helps the police to trace their movements before they died, and can reveal who the last person was to see them alive.

Pathologists can examine four different things to estimate when a person died:

**1** How stiff is the body? Once blood stops pumping through the muscles, they start to get stiff. This is called *rigor mortis*. It begins about three hours after death. Two days later, the muscles relax again, and the body unstiffens.

**2** How warm is the body? Living bodies have a constant temperature of 37°C (98°F). After death, they cool down by about 1° per hour, until they are the same temperature as the room they're in. Pathologists need to know exactly where a body has been since it died. Bodies cool down more quickly under water, for example.

**3** What's in the stomach? It can take more than 30 hours to digest a meal fully. Food passes through the stomach after about two hours, and then sits in the intestines. After death the body stops digesting. So if pathologists find any food, they can guess the length of time between a person's last meal and their death.

**4**. What's in the eyes? Eyeballs contain a small amount of the chemical potassium. After death, the amount of potassium in the eye increases at a steady rate.

If the body is found just a few hours or days after death, all these methods can provide a good idea of the exact time of death. But none of them is perfect. What happens to a body after death depends on where it is, too. Bodies will decompose much more quickly in a hot or wet place, for example.

Pathologists and surgeons use many of the same tools. Here you can see two types of scissors for cutting, and a syringe and kidney dish for collecting samples.

# The telltale pizza

Illinois. USA. 1983. While David Hendricks was on a business trip his wife and three children were found at his home. murdered with an axe. Hendricks soon became the chief suspect. The big question: at exactly what time did Hendricks leave the house?

## Examiners of death

A dead body doesn't always mean there was a murder. Pathologists first try to find the physical cause of death, before trying to work out why it happened. From a medical point of view, people only die when their heart stops beating, or their brain shuts down, or, most commonly, if their lungs stop breathing.

Pathologists can usually determine which of these three events occured first. Then, they may be able to detect an external cause. But this doesn't always give evidence of a crime. Even if a body shows signs of having been attacked, the person might have died of something entirely unconnected, such as an infection.

In some countries pathologists work with people called coroners. It's the coroner's job to decide whether or not a death is suspicious. Coroners don't just look at the body. They also question any witnesses, and they will decide if the witnesses' statements match with the physical evidence left on the body.

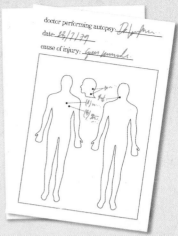

This pathologist's report shows the areas on a body that have been injured, and describes likely causes of those injuries.

### DEATH FACT

When a body is first found, it is carefully photographed by a CSI. Then it is taken to a morgue, where it can be stored in a chilled compartment to prevent it from decomposing before it is examined.

These two technicians are recording the details of a body that has just been delivered to the morgue.

# Pathology on the outside...

The operation to examine a dead body is called an autopsy, or a *post mortem*. Here are some of the things a pathologist might be able to find.

The angle and depth of a wound can reveal what type of weapon was used.

Damage to the skull shows that the head was hit, but you have to look at the brain to see how badly.

Tiny or enlarged pupils often mean that the person has taken drugs, or has been poisoned.

Bruises made by hands or a cord show the victim was strangled.

A tiny hole in the skin is evidence of being injected - by drugs or poison, or air. An air bubble trapped in a vein can kill someone.

Bullet entry wounds are quite small. If they were fired from close range, there will be burn marks around the edge.

After death, blood collects at the bottom of a body, leaving pink marks called lividity marks. These can show the angle a person lay after they died.

# ...and on the inside

If the brain is damaged on the opposite side of the head from a bruise, it means the real damage was from a fall, not a blow to the head.

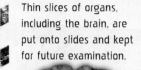

Thin slices of organs, including the brain, are put onto slides and kept for future examination.

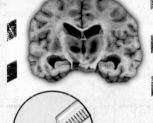

If a person died because of a fire, there would be soot in the lungs.

Blood is tested to see if a person died from an infection.

Bullets can be extracted for testing by ballistics and firearms experts.

Half-digested pieces of food show how long ago the person ate a meal.

If a person drowned in a river or lake, there will be tiny plants called diatoms in the bone marrow. They won't be present if an already dead body was thrown in.

Poisons usually leave traces in hair, bones and some organs.

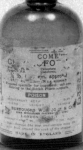

# The wife in the bathtub

**Place:** Bradford, UK

**Date:** 1957

**Crime:** murder

**Victim:** Mrs. Elizabeth Barlow

**Chief suspect:** Kenneth Barlow, nurse

**Incriminating evidence: 1.** Mrs. Barlow drowned in the bathtub. Her husband, a nurse, said he had tried to resuscitate her, but there were no splashes around the room. **2.** Mr. Barlow had been married before; his ex-wife had also died young.

**Suspect's statement:** "I was asleep and didn't go to check on her until it was too late."

**First impression:** not guilty. The pathologist suspected poisoning rather than drowning, but could find no trace of poison.

**Forensic breakthrough:** a thorough examination by two pathologists finally revealed two injection marks in Mrs. Barlow's buttocks. Minute traces of insulin were found in the holes. Insulin is a chemical that the body produces itself. But injecting an extra dose can kill a person...

**Verdict:** guilty

**Sentence:** life in prison

As a nurse, Ken Barlow had easy access to medical supplies, and knew the dangers of insulin poisoning.

# Making faces

Autopsies can be valuable for finding out how and when a person died. But if you don't know the identity of the body, they don't often help to solve the crime.

If no one recognizes the face, or if it is too badly damaged, the first things to look for are any unique markings. Fingerprints and DNA analysis can help, but only if the person was listed on a criminal database. Any tattoos or birthmarks should be noted on a missing persons report. But these will only show up on a fairly well-preserved body.

Victims of a fire may have little left to reveal their identity – beyond teeth and bones. Luckily, these can be helpful, too. Dentists keep very accurate records of teeth, which police can use to compare with teeth found at a crime scene. And, although skulls might look very similar to the untrained eye, experts can tell gender, age and ethnic background just by looking at them. It's also possible to reconstruct a person's face around their skull using clay.

A skull can't reveal everything about a face. Nose shape, skin tone, and hairstyle all have to be guessed at.

## Facial reconstruction

**1**

Pegs are placed to mark out the thickness of muscle and skin.

**2**

Following the pattern of the skull, the face muscles are rebuilt with clay.

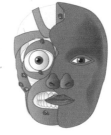

**3**

Glass eyes are put into the sockets, and a layer of fake skin is added over the muscles.

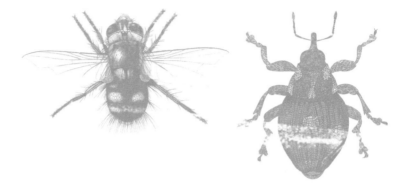

**6**

# Clues from nature

**S**ometimes the best clues about a crime don't come from the people involved, but from the world around them. People up to no good in the woods will disturb the plants and trees, leaving evidence behind. Insects and other animals at the scene of a crime might hold subtle clues.

First on the scene at most murders are not the police, but swarms of flies that eat dead flesh. Experts called entomologists study insects, and they will be called in to examine them.

# A bug's life

CSIs collect samples of maggots, flies, and insect remains that they find on and around a body. To an entomologist, these are clues that can reveal where a body was when a person died, and how long ago they died. Pathologists can only tell the time of death on a newly dead corpse. But entomologists can work on corpses days or even months after death.

First they identify the species of insect. Then, they check what stages of growth each insect is at, for example, maggot, larva or pupa. The variety of stages of insect found show how long ago the person died. They can also tell what time of day a person died, because some insects only come out by day or by night.

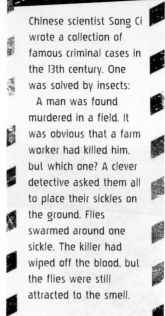

**CRIME FACT**

Chinese scientist Song Ci wrote a collection of famous criminal cases in the 13th century. One was solved by insects:
   A man was found murdered in a field. It was obvious that a farm worker had killed him, but which one? A clever detective asked them all to place their sickles on the ground. Flies swarmed around one sickle. The killer had wiped off the blood, but the flies were still attracted to the smell.

Bluebottles and blowflies like to lay their eggs on very fresh bodies.

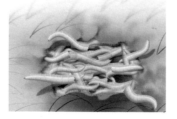

Maggots hatch in a few hours. Over the next week, they grow and change.

Finally, the maggots make cocoons next to the body. After twelve days, they emerge as adult flies.

These are some of the most common insects found on dead bodies near to towns.

A springtail maggot

An adult bluebottle fly

An adult blowfly

Insects live all over the world, in almost every kind of environment. Forensic entomologists can use this fact to help the police solve certain crimes, such as smuggling.

Smugglers bring illegal goods from one part of the world to another. Insects often get into the packing crates they use, and travel around the world with them. Entomologists can look at these insects and tell exactly where the crates have come from, helping police to tackle the crime at its source.

## Crime against animals

People kill animals for food, clothing, and in some cases, medicine. In the last hundred years, scientists have learned that many species will die out completely if we don't protect them. So, in most countries it is illegal to kill rare animals, even if they can be used to make useful things.

Since the discovery of DNA profiling, it is easy for scientists to prove what species a sample of fur or bone powder comes from, making life harder for illegal hunters and traders.

## Man's best friends?

Experts can train certain breeds of dog to hunt for missing people by giving them a scent to follow. These are known as sniffer dogs. They can also be used to find other things with a distinctive smell, such as illegal drugs. Trained dogs can help CSIs to look for traces of a suspect or certain types of chemicals at a crime scene. A forensic scientist examines the things sniffer dogs uncover, to find out what they are.

Dogs aren't the only creatures with a strong sense of smell. Scientists have discovered that, in just a few hours, they can train a swarm of wasps to sniff out drugs and chemicals used to make bombs. The wasps will hover menacingly above a suspect...

# Getting dirty

Insects can show how long a body has been dead, but they won't often be able to help find the criminal responsible. Luckily, nature hides plenty of other clues. Leaves, seeds and soil get stuck to people very easily, especially to the soles of their shoes.

Soil can be found in a wide variety of textures and shades. Looking at the details makes it possible to match soil from a shoe with soil from a particular place.

Diatoms are incredibly small plants that live in water. Soil with diatoms in it probably comes from a place by a stream or river.

Chemists use litmus paper to test the acidity of soil. Some soils are more acidic than others.

Plant seeds often stick to a shoe, or are found in soil on a shoe. A plant expert called a botanist can tell where they have come from.

Different types of soil look different, even to the naked eye. This gritty soil isn't found everywhere.

A thorough CSI should take careful samples of soil and the things hidden in it from the area around a crime scene. Later on, these can be compared to samples of dirt and soil found on a suspect's clothes and shoes. If an expert finds enough matching material in the two samples, this can be used as evidence in court.

Under a powerful microscope, it's possible to find bacteria hidden in soil. These can be traced to a particular area.

# Proof in the pollen

**Name:** Dr. Patricia Wiltshire

**Base of operations:** United Kingdom, present day

**Occupation:** forensic botanist

**Methods:** Dr. Wiltshire scours crime scenes and dead bodies to look for tiny remains of plants, especially seeds and pollen. She will insert a special stick into the corpse's nose, which is a great place to find pollen grains. Her detective skills have earned her an international reputation as a crime-solver.

**Recent case:** Well Wood, UK, and Tirana, Albania 2004.

**Crime:** murder of Dritan Perdoda

**Clue 1:** the body was found in a grave that had been carefully dug out. The grave site contained remains of unusual types of pollen.

**Chief suspect:** Ritzvan Matranxhi, a man who had entrusted money to Perdoda, and who had recently fled from the UK to his home town of Tirana, capital of Albania.

**Clue 2:** Dr. Wiltshire flew out to Tirana, and searched Matranxhi's car – a car registered in the UK. Sure enough, she found traces of the same type of pollen as in the grave in Well Wood.

**Verdict:** guilty

**Sentence:** 23 years in prison

Pollen from different plants looks different under a microscope. Pollen experts are called palynologists.

# Reading wood

Plants aren't only useful to detectives when they're found in the wild. Even after a tree has been cut down, treated, and made into furniture, it still contains plenty of clues.

Every year that a tree grows, a visible line appears in its trunk, known as a growth ring. Every tree that grows in the same forest will have similar growth rings, but examined up close they are as unique as human fingerprints. Experts called dendrochronologists can tell how old a tree is – and where in the world it has come from – by examining growth rings. These growth rings are visible in furniture, where they are seen as lines called wood grain.

Furniture can often have other markings, too. Old wood can attract woodworm, which chew out tiny tunnels in it. Stains from dyes that carpenters use leave a chemical trace. Forensic scientists can examine these details on even a tiny splinter. For example, splinters of wood found on a victim can be traced to a wooden bat owned by a suspect. This kind of evidence is known as fragmentary evidence.

## FAKE FACT

A famous violin called the Messiah hangs in the Ashmolean museum in the UK. It is said to be the work of renowned violin maker Stradivarius. In 1998, an expert examined the growth rings on the violin and declared that the tree it was made from was cut down in 1730 – several years after Stradivarius died. But other experts disagree with this dating.

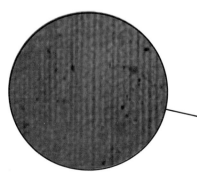

The grain visible in this violin can be examined by a dendrochronologist. They will be able to tell how old the wood is, and can even guess when the tree was cut down.

# Hair, seeds, dust and fungus

Most murders are committed by people who already know their victim. But when someone famous is killed, it can be very hard to narrow down a list of suspects. Read this story to see how Australian forensic scientists used a whole variety of clues from nature to pinpoint just one man.

ON JUNE 1ST, 1960, THE THORNE FAMILY WON THE FIRST AUSTRALIAN LOTTERY.

THAT MONEY SHOULD BE MINE!

NOT EVERYONE WAS HAPPY ABOUT THIS...

8 YEAR-OLD GRAEME WAS KIDNAPPED A MONTH LATER.

POOR GRAEME WAS FOUND DEAD SIX WEEKS LATER, WRAPPED IN A BLANKET.

THE KIDNAPPER MADE HIS DEMANDS...

GIMME $25,000 OR ELSE!

...BUT WAS NOT HEARD FROM AGAIN.

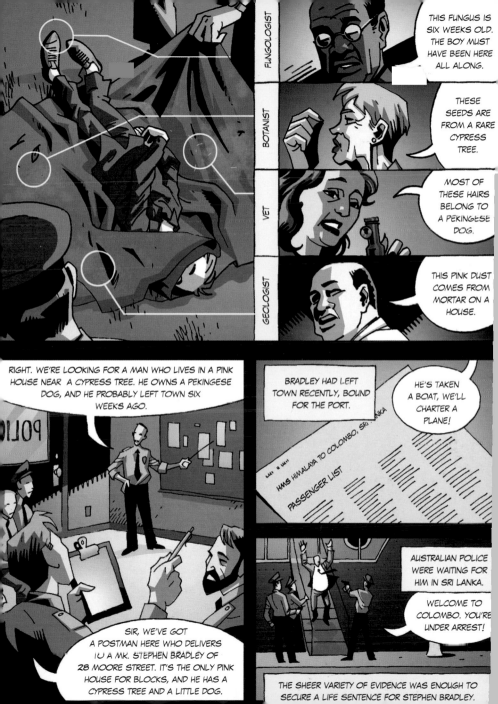

# CHAPTER 7
# The little things

It's said that no two snowflakes look alike. But this isn't so amazing – if you examine anything up close, it's almost impossible to find two things that look exactly alike.

Take two same-value coins. Even though they were made by the same machine, you can easily tell them apart if you look carefully. Over time, coins pick up dirt and scratches that make them more and more different. This happens to all kinds of things, and these unique markings can help to solve a crime.

# Through the magnifying glass

The magnifying glass has been the classic symbol for a detective in crime novels and films for over a hundred years. This simple tool is still used by CSIs to hunt for small clues. But to magnify the details on objects of all sizes, microscopes are the tool of choice in a crime lab. Forensic scientists of all specialities use them, from pathologists to experts on tools and glass.

Tiny specks of glass and metal are out of place in these woods. Where did they come from?

Small strands of cloth might have belonged to the criminal's clothes or gloves.

Wheel tracks reveal what kind of car was being driven. They might even have their own unique patterns.

This mark in the ground is unique to the shovel that was used here.

## Crime Scene: body in the woods

After he's finished burying his victim, the criminal will pick up his shovel and drive off. He's confident that the police will not suspect him. He doesn't realize that this crime scene is full of tiny traces that forensic scientists can analyze...

A pair of tweezers is used to collect a tiny thread. A microscope will reveal exactly what it is.

FORENSIC FACT

Strands from hair or clothing look very different under a microscope.

Hair from a house cat

Polyester from a shirt

Wool from a sweater

# Fragment puzzles

Anything from a tiny shard of glass to a thread of green cloth might turn out to be the vital clue in cracking a case. Criminals often leave these clues behind because they can't see them. And many people don't realize how much information forensic scientists can get out of these fragments using modern technology.

Powerful microscopes can show things in such detail that an expert can see what material something is made from, and uncover any unique impurities in that particular object.

Broken glass, for example, is common at many crime scenes. CSIs sometimes also find glass shards in a suspect's house, or on their clothes, or in their car. Detectives send all these shards to a glass expert, to find out if they all come from the same windowpane.

Glass is not unique in the same way as DNA, but there are many variations for experts to find by examining the texture and thickness. An expert can study glass shards by shining a light through them, and then say if all the shards came from the same windowpane.

Even if CSIs only find glass at the scene of the crime, the same tests can reveal to an expert where this type of glass was made. Then, a detective can contact the companies that make it, trace every shop that sells it, and start investigating their customers. It's a slow method, but it often helps to identify a suspect – particularly if the glass is rare.

# Every contact leaves a trace

**Name:** Edmund Locard

**Base of operations:** France, 1895-1966

**Occupation:** professor of forensic medicine

**Methods:** Locard pioneered a principle that has become central to all of forensic science – the exchange principle. It is the observation that people leave traces behind and pick up traces wherever they go. With this in mind, Locard routinely inspected crime scenes and suspects to look for tiny clues.

**Classic case:** Lyon, France, 1921

**Crime:** murder by strangulation of Marie Latelle

**Chief suspect:** Emile Gourbin, Marie's boyfriend

**Clue 1:** Locard scraped some muck out of Gourbin's fingernails, and examined it under a microscope. He found traces of skin, blood, and a pink powder.

**Clue 2:** Marie's bedroom contained a box full of the same pink powder: it was part of her makeup kit.

**Confession:** Gourbin was so astonished at what Locard found that he admitted he had strangled Marie.

**Verdict:** guilty

**Sentence:** death

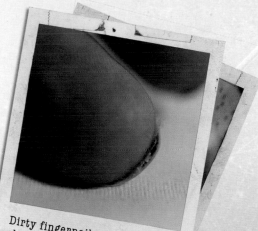

Dirty fingernails are a mine of clues about a person's recent activities. It pays to keep clean!

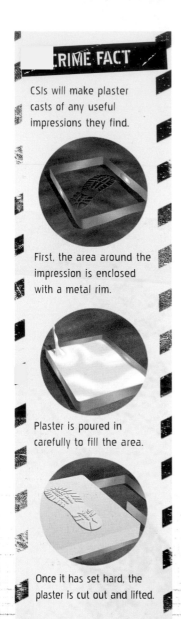

CSIs will make plaster casts of any useful impressions they find.

First, the area around the impression is enclosed with a metal rim.

Plaster is poured in carefully to fill the area.

Once it has set hard, the plaster is cut out and lifted.

## A lasting impression

Forensic scientists don't even need an actual object to examine. They can also obtain information by looking at the impressions an object leaves in the ground, on a building, or even on a person. Experts can examine a shoe print or a wheel track to find its unique markings, which can then be matched to the shoe or car wheel that left the impression. CSIs will take a plaster cast of such impressions to send to experts and to use as evidence in court.

## Teeth and tool marks

When people bite down on something, their teeth leave a unique pattern. It's the same with tools, such as saws, hammers or bolt cutters. These kinds of tools all work by grinding against an object until it breaks. Sometimes, the tool will get a tiny amount of damage to its cutting edge, which gives it a unique 'tooth mark' the next time it cuts something. These marks are easy to see under a powerful microscope.

The scratches on this screwdriver will leave unique marks on any doors a burglar uses it to force open.

To double-check that a mark was made by a particular tool, a scientist will use the tool on a test object, to see if it leaves exactly the same teeth marks.

## Forensic databases

Every kind of tool leaves a unique mark after it's used. Sometimes the impressions are too faint or dirty to be studied properly. And unless detectives have a suspicious tool to compare the markings with, close examination can't help them solve a crime. In this situation, it's the things about tools that are not so unique that can be helpful. Even a faint impression can be enough to reveal what kind of tool was used, giving detectives a way into an investigation.

Dedicated forensic scientists have spent years using different types of tools on different surfaces. They take a photo of each mark, and file them in a huge database. In a similar way, wheel and shoe manufacturers add pictures of all their designs to police databases.

The idea is that fellow forensic scientists can access these databases to look for photos that match marks found at a crime scene. Many marks can be linked to one specific model and brand of tool. It's then possible to trace that brand from the factory it was made in to the shops where it was sold, in the same way as using glass evidence.

### TEETH FACT

Human and animal teeth also leave marks on the things they bite. Scientists who specialize in studying tooth evidence are called forensic odontologists.

Two murderers, Ted Bundy and Gordon Hay, were both found guilty in court as a result of bite marks they'd left on their victims. Odontologists compared the marks with their teeth, and found a positive match.

Fast-changing fashions are a great help to detectives. Many shoe manufacturers change the style of their shoe soles every few months, so it's easy to tell when a shoe was bought. New sole patterns are automatically loaded into a dalabase.

# The hacksaw horror

In 1981, Mrs. Leah Rosenthal was reported missing. She had just been to visit her son Danny in Southampton, UK. Danny seemed very unconcerned about his mother, which made the police suspicious. Danny's father Milton lived in France, and detectives hoped he could help. Instead, the plot thickened...

SAYCE AND SIMS PROVED THAT THE HACKSAW BLADE FOUND IN MILTON ROSENTHAL'S APARTMENT HAD BEEN USED TO CUT THE LEG FROM THE RIVER. DANNY WAS FOUND GUILTY, AND WAS SENT TO A PSYCHIATRIC PRISON FOR TREATMENT.

**8**

# Going ballistic

The noise of a gunshot is loud enough and rare enough in many parts of the world that unexpected bangs are reported and investigated by the police, even if it turns out that no crime has been committed. Police officers have to write careful reports about every shot they fire.

The science of how bullets move through the air is called ballistics. It's common to refer to any forensic work involving guns and bullets as ballistics, although police officers and experts also call it firearms investigation.

Most guns work in the same way. Pulling the trigger makes a small hammer smack into the the bullet case. A mixture of chemicals inside the bullet case then explodes, forcing the bullet to fly out of the gun. The bullet moves faster than the speed of sound, so it makes a bang.

This all leaves lots of evidence after a shooting incident: used bullets, empty bullet cases, chemical residue from the bullet, bullet holes and of course the guns used. A firearms expert uses these clues to solve different problems: which bullets came from which gun, who was holding a gun, or where they shot from.

## GUN FACT

Guns are one example of a larger group of weapons called firearms. Any weapon that uses a propellant to shoot out objects at high speed is classed as a firearm. As well as all kinds of guns, this includes some spray cans, that 'shoot' dangerous liquids such as pepper spray.

## Anatomy of a gun

This kind of gun is a semiautomatic. After each shot, it pushes an empty case out of the top of the gun, and moves a new round into the firing position.

Gun barrel    Bullet    Case    Firing pin

Trigger

Spare rounds

Bullet rounds are made up of several different parts:

The actual bullet is the round piece at the top.

The bullet is held inside an outer shell called the case.

Beneath the bullet is an explosive chemical called a propellant.

At the bottom of the round is a chemical primer that sets off the propellant.

A bullet case often has a serial number stamped on it.

Detectives can use this to trace where a bullet was made and bought.

The firing pin of a gun leaves a unique mark on each case.

## Which gun was used?

The police won't always find a gun at the scene of a shooting, but it's rare for them not to find bullet holes and bullets. Ballistics experts can tell what type of gun was used by looking at the bullets. Bullets need to fit very snugly inside a gun, so many guns only work when using the right type of bullet. When they are fired, grooves inside the gun barrel, known as rifling, leave marks called striations on each bullet.
 The firing pin leaves a small hole in the bullet case, too. A gun will leave exactly the same markings on every bullet and case that it fires. So, to prove that a particular gun was used to fire a particular bullet, a firearms expert simply fires off a round using the suspect gun. Then he or she can examine the two bullets and the two cases. If the markings on both bullets and cases match, they must have been fired from the same gun. Some bullets are too mangled to see the striation marks on them, but used cases

After they hit their target, bullets get squashed. How much they get squashed depends on how far away and how hard the target is. Ballistics experts can estimate how far away a shot came from by how much a bullet is squashed.

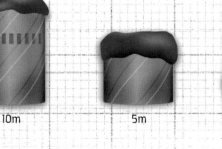

20m     10m     5m     1m

always have a visible firing pin mark. A shooter has to collect them if he or she doesn't want to get caught.

In 1923, an amazingly useful forensic tool called the comparison microscope was invented specifically to compare two bullets. The bullets are placed on a slide, and the examiner looks through a single hole to see close-ups of them side by side. This way, the examiner can easily compare the markings on both bullets to see whether or nor they match up. This microscope is useful to many branches of forensic science.

## Who fired the gun?

When a trigger is pulled, the primer in the back of the bullet reacts with the propellant, causing an explosion. It also creates new gases which spit out of a hole in the top of the gun. These gases are called gunshot residues.

Anyone who has held or fired a gun can have traces of residue on their clothes and hands. The primer and propellant in the bullet round both create gases. Guns themselves can also leave residue on a person from the oil used to keep them working. CSIs will use a treated swab to wipe the hands of any suspect as soon as they can. The swab can be tested to see if it has any gun residues on it. However, gun residues are all very similar, so swab tests can't prove which gun a suspect used.

**CRIME FACT**

In 1838, William Stewart became the first person in America to be sent to prison because of ballistic evidence.

He was accused of murdering his father to get a quick inheritance. At the autopsy, a number of round bullets were found. These unusual bullets were sent to a local gunsmith, who recognized them. He had made them himself, especially for William Stewart's gun.

A swab picks up traces of dirt on a person's hands. A special dye turns purple if the dirt contains any gun residue.

# Reconstructing a gun battle

Last night this New York diner was the scene of a gun battle. Two police officers (in blue) chased a gang of three criminals (in red) to the diner. A detective will try to match up the evidence found at the scene with statements given by the survivors.

The position and angle of the hole in this door and the wall behind it show where the shot was fired from.

CSIs try to find every bullet that was fired. The easiest place to start looking is inside a bullet hole.

After shooting, some guns will automatically eject the case that the bullet was in. At this scene, the positions of the empty cases show that this police officer moved in between firing his shots.

The angle of a bullet hole can show the direction the bullet was moving in. CSIs use string to mark out the path that every bullet took as it flew. Here, it provides another clue pinpointing where the police officer stood.

Every gun found will be checked to see if it was used. Then detectives will try to find out what happened to every bullet fired from them.

Different bullets leave different types of marks on the things they hit. Experts will match each bullet to the gun that fired it.

Blood spatter patterns on the wall show which direction the shot came from.

These bullets haven't been fired yet. It looks as if this gang member tried to reload his weapon here.

## Crime scene: gun battle in a diner

Two of the gang members were killed, and one police officer was injured. The third gang member surrendered. The detective who analyzed the scene also worked out the following facts:

- Only three guns were used – two people were shot before they could fire.
- One police officer managed to shoot one of the gang members from outside the bar. She then rushed into the bar where she shot one man, and forced a third man to surrender. She counted the number of shots fired, and knew that she could enter and shoot while the others reloaded.

nobleman. She liked to have a good time, and didn't like being let down by her boyfriends. Put a gun in her hands, and anything could happen – even murder. But proving it in 1932 was all too difficult...

**9.**

# Exploding evidence

**I**f it's hot enough, fire can reduce nearly
everything in its path to ash and soot. Because
of this, all kinds of crime can involve fire. Wily
criminals hope that a fire will disguise or
destroy evidence of their crimes. And terrorists
set off explosions, as well as starting fires, to try
to cause as much damage as possible.

Luckily, fires do eventually go out, and
explosions never destroy everything. It's always
possible to find some clues about how they
started and, if it was deliberate, who started it.

Fires and explosions nearly always start in one place, known as the seat. As a rule, they travel up and spread out. So an expert can guess where a fire or explosion started by working back through a trail of burned-out debris.

Finding the seat of a fire makes it easier to work out how the fire started. Someone who starts a fire deliberately might be trying to destroy one thing in particular, probably near the seat. It's part of the painstaking work of the investigator to check on everything that was destroyed, and try to discover what it was before the fire burned it. For example, remnants of a document might help to pinpoint the culprit.

## CRIME FACT

Starting a fire in order to damage someone else's property is a crime commonly known as arson. After any major fire, investigators will look for any evidence of arson.

Some criminals commit arson on their own possessions hoping to get money from an insurance policy.

## Starting fires

Fires are the result of a chemical reaction between oxygen and fuels such as wood. There has to be enough heat for this reaction to begin, but once a fire starts, it will keep on burning as long as it has enough air and fuel.

Some fuels react much more strongly than others. Wood is a fine fuel for a bonfire, but it takes a while to catch alight. To start a fire really quickly, it's common to use gasoline, alcohol or another flammable liquid. These can be poured onto the ground or all over a room and lit easily with a match. Chemicals like these are called accelerants. If a CSI finds any traces of accelerants at the scene of a fire, it's likely that the fire wasn't an accident.

Accelerants can be found in some common household items such as paint thinners. They should be stored in watertight containers, so they don't spill by accident.

# After a fire

Firefighters have the job of saving lives and putting out any fires they are called to. It's also part of their job to find out what caused a fire as soon as possible. Evidence of a deliberate fire can disappear if it's not found quickly. Finding the cause of an accidental fire is important, too, as it can help prevent a similar fire elsewhere.

Fire burns up and fans out. This creates a 'V' shape of soot and burned areas. The bottom of the V shows where the fire started.

This warehouse is virtually empty. Detectives will be suspicious if the owner removed the goods recently.

The fire smashed this window. Then the air sucked the flames to the right.

Trained sniffer dogs known as 'accelerant detection canines' help search for suspect chemicals.

A trail on the ground has been heavily burned. This kind of mark is often caused by spilled accelerant.

# Anatomy of a bomb

Like deliberate fires, bombs use special chemicals that can catch fire or explode easily. Bombs all have the same parts, but each can be made from different things.

This is the main charge, in this case made of plastic explosive. It reacts with the detonator to produce an explosion.

A home-made bomb is sometimes called an Improvised Explosive Device, or IED.

A control device is used to set off the bomb. Here, the device is in two parts.

The phone sends a signal to this receiver which is attached directly to the bomb.

The control device then activates this detonator. It contains a chemical that can explode easily.

Bombs can be made with different kinds of detonators. Some are activated from a distance by a signal from a phone, or by a lit fuse connected directly to the main charge. Others can be equipped with a timer switch, or a switch that turns on when the bomb is moved.

The part that explodes is described as the main charge. This can be made from any kind of chemical that reacts with the detonator. This reaction makes a loud noise, and creates new gases, which expand quickly and push against anything that stands in their way. This blast of gases, called a shockwave, can be strong enough to twist metal and break concrete.

## BOMB FACT

This x-ray picture shows a homemade bomb hidden inside an envelope. Guards in high security buildings always check bags for bombs.

## After a bomb

Explosions don't burn things up, unless the gases in them happen to start a fire. They usually smash things into tiny pieces, spread them out over a huge area and make a mess. Bomb investigators spend hours sifting through the debris to find fragments from the bomb, that can help reveal how it was made.

These fragments were found on the ground after a bomb went off in a plane. On the right are some tiny pieces of metal from the bomb itself. On the left are pieces of cloth and paper that the bomb was wrapped in.

### CSI FACT

Objects like bricks, wood and cloth found near a fire or explosion can absorb propellant gases. CSIs keep samples in airtight jars to stop the gases from evaporating.

## Chemical analysis

Chemicals are all made up of different parts called molecules, that make different chemicals behave in different ways. The main challenge for a forensic chemistry expert is to work out exactly what is in any chemical residues found at the scene of a fire or explosion. To help them do this, many use a machine called a Gas Chromatograph-Mass Spectrometer (GC-MS).

First, it produces a gas chromatogram. This is a chart which shows a pattern made by each chemical in the sample. Experts study the patterns to identify what kind of chemicals they are, for example a dangerous accelerant.

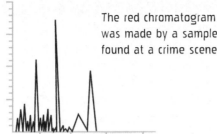

The red chromatogram was made by a sample found at a crime scene.

The blue chromatogram was made by residue found on a suspect's hands.

The peaks do not match, so the suspect is free to go.

Next, the GC-MS tests and identifies the gases to reveal the combination of molecules they are made from. By studying the chromatogram and the spectrometer result, the expert knows exactly which chemicals were found at the crime scene.

This information can prove that a fire or explosion was deliberate. For example, some chemicals – such as RDX – were developed specifically to be used in bombs. Traces of RDX found at a bomb site or on a suspect's hands are a strong indication that the bombing was planned in advance.

The test might also find that a common household chemical caused a fire. This might mean that the fire was an accident, but it's important to check the suspects. Swabs taken from their clothes and hands will be tested by GC-MS. If experts find traces of the same chemical residues, the detectives involved in the case will want to know how they got there.

**CRIME FACT**

Up until the 20th century, poisoning was the most popular way to commit murder and get away with it.

Throughout the 18th and 19th centuries, doctors and chemists found ways to identify certain poisons in a dead body, or from a suspicious glass of wine.

Nowadays, GC-MS analysis can identify even the most obscure poison from a victim or crime scene sample. Sadly, people still try to get away with murder, but they no longer trust poison to hide it.

# The Birmingham Six

**Place:** Birmingham, UK

**Date:** 1974

**Crime:** setting off two terrorist bombs

**Victims:** 21 killed, 162 wounded

**Chief suspects:** six men who were arrested leaving the area on the morning after the bombing.

**Suspects' statement:** "We were on our way home for a friend's funeral. We don't know anything about the bombs."

**Incriminating evidence:** a noted forensic scientist performed a 'Greiss' test on the six suspects to check for bomb residues. He found that two of them had traces of nitroglycerin – an explosive chemical – on their hands. Five of the six then confessed to the bombing under gruelling interrogation.

**Verdict:** guilty

**Forensic breakthrough:** the 'Greiss' test was shown to be unreliable. A GC-MS test found no trace of any explosive chemicals. Photographic evidence proved that the suspects had been beaten up in order to make them confess. Sadly, it took 16 years to get back to court.

**Appeal verdict:** not guilty

The Greiss test does detect nitro glycerin, but it also detects other common (and harmless) chemicals.

# CHAPTER 10
# The paper trail

There are some kinds of crime that don't have a crime scene. For example, thieves can steal money from peoples' bank accounts over the internet. A letter or a phone call can be criminal, if it's a death threat. Criminals called forgers can make fake money and try to spend it.

These crimes can still be solved. Some forensic experts can find clues in paper and ink, including money. Others find clues by following a trail of evidence left behind on paper documents and computer files.

All paper money is printed in special and highly secure factories called mints. It is designed to be impossible to copy, but criminals still like to try. Luckily for the police, there are usually a number of obvious ways to tell whether a banknote or bill is real or not.

Every banknote in the world has a unique serial number.

Special printing techniques mean that money cannot be photocopied or scanned onto a computer.

A thin strip of metal is squeezed between the layers.

Many notes are printed using ink that changes shade when light shines on it at different angles.

## Forensic accounting

Banks keep a record of the money that goes into and out of every account. If a criminal steals money electronically, it can be traced using these records. Accountants follow a trail that can reveal the criminal's address, and shows where they have spent the stolen money.

Accountants are also called in to help with a crime almost as old as murder – tax evasion. Most people pay tax to the government depending on how much they earn. But some people try to hide their money so that they don't have to pay as much tax as they should.

Anyone suspected of doing this can be investigated by accountants. They search computer and paper files to work out how much how a person earns and how much tax they should pay. Anyone not paying enough can be fined or even arrested.

## Whose signature?

Pretending to be someone else, known as fraud, can be a serious crime. Criminals don't have to be great actors to do this. They just need to produce a document signed in someone else's name. This is an easy way to get someone else's money. To foil this crime, detectives ask expert document examiners to check suspicious papers.

**CRIME FACT**

In the 1920s, gangster Al Capone led a wave of crime in Chicago, USA, but the police couldn't find enough evidence to arrest him. Then, in 1931, a forensic accountant found Capone's private ledger. He proved in court that Capone had not been paying his taxes. Capone went to prison.

This letter has a signature at the bottom that the police know is genuine.

Most people's signatures look a little different each time they sign something. This signature comes from a suspicious document. Could it be too similar to the original?

A document examiner has overlaid the two signatures. It looks as if the suspect signature was traced – so it's a forgery.

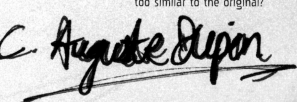

## INK FACT

As well as checking the handwriting, experts can also examine the paper and ink used.

Shining certain kinds of light onto a document can show when it has been tampered with.

This image shows the date on a person's driving license.

Under ultraviolet light, it's easy to see that part of the date was written in a different kind of ink. It's possible that the owner has tampered with it to make himself or herself older or younger – a type of fraud.

Experts also examine the way each letter has been formed and joined together. Certain features tend to be the same each time a person writes or signs something. For example, left- and right-handed people often move their pens in different directions when writing. Also, the writing of an older person can be a lot more spidery than a younger person's, making it hard for them to forge each other accurately.

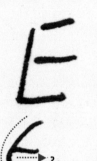

There are at least three common ways to write a capital letter 'E'. Look at the examples below and see which one you think best matches this sample.

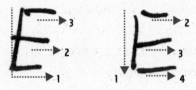

Looking at where the pen has been lifted off the paper, the middle sample seems to be the best match. In real life, experts will look for many other details, using a microscope. They will compare a suspect sample with at least six genuine samples.

## Hidden in paper

Writing with a pen doesn't just leave an ink mark. It also leaves an impression on the piece of paper, and if there were other sheets underneath, there will be impressions on them, too. You can sometimes see these kinds of impressions by tilting the paper up to the light. A machine called an Electro-Static Detection Apparatus (ESDA) can display these impressions even if they're very faint.

In normal light, it's possible to see the writing impressions on this blank sheet of paper, but they are too faint to read.

ESDA can highlight the impressions and produce a clear printout. This is part of a ransom letter written by a kidnapper.

A criminal who burns away any written evidence about his crime might not think to burn a whole pad of blank paper. ESDA can help detectives to find all kinds of clues left on blank pads found at a crime scene, such as a name or phone number.

If the impressions found on a pad of paper match up with writing on a suspicious document, such as a death threat, then the owner of the pad will have some difficult questions to answer.

## Electronic traces

People still use signatures as a way to keep documents official. But it's becoming more common to store important information on a computer, and to use electronic protection such as passwords or Personal Identification Numbers (PINs) to keep things safe.

## CRIME FACT

In 1991 in the East Midlands, UK, a man went into a bank and handed over a note. It said he'd shoot someone if he wasn't given money. The robber went out with his loot, but he left the note behind.

A document expert checked the note using ESDA, and found impressions of a long list of drinks. Police officers went to a store near to the bank, and the manager recognized the list as a customer's order. Armed with his address, the police arrested the customer, who soon confessed.

CRIME FACT

**Microchips** from all kinds of things can be analyzed by experts

**Digital cameras** contain memory chips that might reveal a suspect's face or friends

**Printers** and photocopiers have a memory chip that can be used to reprint the last few documents.

**Credit cards** have a chip that records where and when they have been used.

Over the last two decades, a new kind of crime has become all too common – electronic fraud. People who know how to use computers, especially the Internet, can pretend to be other people. They hack into personal computers to steal information, and can use this to log into a person's bank account and take all their money.

Forensic computer scientists have to stay one step ahead of computer criminals. Luckily, there is often plenty of evidence for them to examine. Every time a person uses any computer, a record is stored on that computer's hard drive to show what commands were given, and when. To most people, these commands are a string of gibberish, but experts can understand them.

Even when the memory on a computer is deleted, the information can still be found inside, until new information is put into the computer, or if it is physically destroyed. Scientists can examine a computer's circuits to identify the most recent instructions, and they can sometimes recover the most recently deleted files. Searching through data to try to find useful evidence is a science in itself, known as information retrieval.

Other kinds of forensic computer experts spend their time on the Internet. They can monitor suspicious or illegal websites to find out who is running them. They can also examine suspects' computers to see what websites they have been looking at, for example to find out if they are part of a terrorist group.

# The hapless thief

Many modern phones are equipped with a Global Positioning System (GPS) receiver. This is a chip that the owner can activate to tell them exactly where they are in the world. It also makes for a handy way to search for a phone if it goes missing, as US ambassador John Beyrle discovered in a Bulgarian airport in 2005...

# CHAPTER 11

# Criminal identity

**M**ost criminal investigations have two main aims: to find out who committed a crime, and to find enough proof to secure a conviction in a court of law.

Physical traces such as blood can prove that a person was in a particular place at a particular time, but it can't show what they were doing there. It's easier for lawyers if they have evidence that shows a person's face, or describes a person's character. This helps juries to decide whether someone is guilty or innocent.

An easy way to prove that someone was at the scene of a crime is to find video footage from the right time and place. A really lucky detective might even find the suspect actually committing the crime on that video.

Cameras are found in all types of places nowadays: inside banks, shops and even along busy roads. Many people use their mobile phones to take pictures and videos. Anyone seen in a photograph or video at the time a crime happened might be able to help the police. But video and photo evidence can be falsified, so it's important for the police to check it carefully.

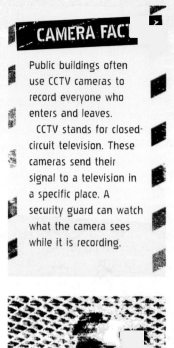

**CAMERA FACT**

Public buildings often use CCTV cameras to record everyone who enters and leaves.

CCTV stands for closed-circuit television. These cameras send their signal to a television in a specific place. A security guard can watch what the camera sees while it is recording.

Most recordings are stored for several days before being deleted. They often display the exact time and date that the video footage was taken.

This man has been caught on camera stealing from a handbag.

An expert will check the video footage to look for a picture that shows the whole of the person's face.

Computers can clean up grainy video images. Then it's easier to identify the person.

## Voice prints

Along with video footage, recordings of a person's voice can be used to prove their guilt. When someone speaks into a microphone, a computer can translate the sound of their voice into a graph called a voice print. Even people who sound very similar have different voice prints. Expert analysts can match up the graph of a suspect's voice with a recording of a voice that relates to a crime – for example a kidnapper's telephone call.

This is a voice print of a person speaking a short sentence. The height of the lines shows the pitch. How close together the lines are shows the tone.

## Forensic psychology

A person's identifying features don't only show up in outward things such as their face or voice. They are also buried inside people's minds. The way a person behaves is a unique marker, so a criminal can be found out by their habits.

Psychologists are scientists who study the human mind. Forensic psychologists study the personalities of people who commit crimes.

Some criminals commit the same kind of crime time and again, and they tend to use the same methods each time. Police use the latin phrase *modus operandi* (often shortened to MO) to describe this habit. It simply means

**FORENSIC FACT**

Psychologists often examine criminals to see if they have a mental illness.

If someone commits a crime because they are ill, they may be sent to a hospital, not to prison.

However, most crimes are committed by sane people.

way of working. Detectives can recognize a criminal's MO based on the time and place the crime occured, and any evidence left by the tools that were used.

A forensic psychologist can analyze what an MO reveals about the criminal involved. Along with any other evidence from a crime scene, they can put together a "personality profile" of the criminal. This profile can include accurate guesses about their height and weight, as well as things about their character and lifestyle.

Forensic psychologists are often the last people to get called in to solve a case. When the police are baffled by a series of crimes that seem to be related, a psychologist can help them to guess what kind of person to look for.

## Crime scene: killer around town

Six murders have been reported in this town. Detectives are trying to work out if they are connected. Information from the scene of each crime might reveal clues about the killer or killers.

- ● Bodies discovered
- ● Weapon found
- ○ Known crime scene
- ● Victims' homes

All the victims were attacked near their offices. Psychologists guess from this that the killer followed them for a few days before deciding the best time to attack.

The bodies were all found close together, and in out-of-the way spots. The killer probably has a car to carry the bodies away in.

Likely murder weapons were found discarded close to the scene of three attacks.

The victims lived all around the town. It's likely the killer lived somewhere near the middle of the town.

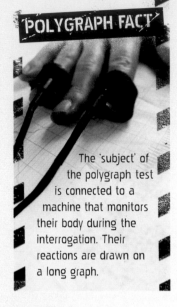

**POLYGRAPH FACT**

The 'subject' of the polygraph test is connected to a machine that monitors their body during the interrogation. Their reactions are drawn on a long graph.

## Interrogation techniques

Police officers are trained to interview witnesses and suspects. This is often called an interrogation. Interrogators have to guess whether or not a person is lying to them, and then try to make them tell the truth.

Psychologists have observed that people's bodies react in different ways when they tell lies. They sweat more, and their heart beats faster. Polygraphs or "lie-detector" machines can measure how a person's body reacts during an interrogation. Experts can watch these responses to see if a person is lying.

The green line measures breathing rate.

The blue line show how much a person is sweating.

The red line measures heart rate.

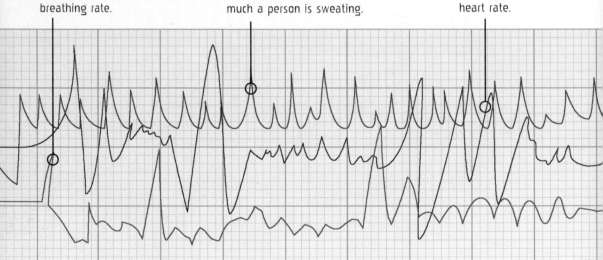

A large blip in one or more of the graphs can indicate a lie – or it might just mean the person was suddenly nervous or in pain.

Sometimes people taking the test are so nervous that their bodies show a strong reaction even when they're telling the truth. Lie-detector tests are not perfect, and are only rarely used in court. But they are still useful to interrogators.

# Crime-solving scientists No. 3
## Secrets in the brain

**Name:** Dr. Lawrence Farwell

**Base of operations:** United States of America, present day

**Occupation:** psychologist

**Methods:** Farwell invented the concept of brain fingerprinting. Whenever a person recognizes something, their brain releases electrical impulses known as P300 brain waves. These can be recorded by connecting an EEG machine to a person's head while showing them pictures.

**Recent case:** Omaha, Nebraska, 2001.

**Crime:** 1977 murder of John Schweer, security guard.

**Chief suspect:** Terry Harrington, teenager.

**Case history:** Harrington claimed he had been at a rock concert, but one of his friends was a witness and said he had seen Harrington shoot Schweer.

**Verdict:** guilty

**Forensic breakthrough:** in 2000, Farwell showed Harrington photos from the crime scene, and from the concert. His brain only released P300 brain waves when he saw photos from the concert. His friend also admitted that he had lied in court to save himself.

**Appeal verdict:** not guilty

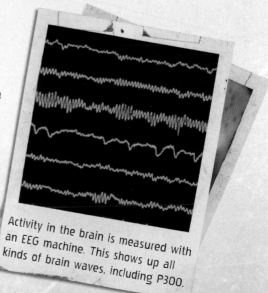

Activity in the brain is measured with an EEG machine. This shows up all kinds of brain waves, including P300.

# "He made me do it!"

Sometimes the mind can be manipulated to make a person do something they normally wouldn't. In Denmark in 1951, an astonishing case came before criminal psychologist Dr. Max Schmidt. The case of Palle Hardrup and the hypnotist...

# Timeline of forensic science

Stories of crime-solving science go back as far as ancient Rome and ancient China. But, since the start of the 19th century, detectives have paid close attention to advances in science. Here are some of the key scientific breakthroughs that have made it easier to solve crimes.

## Forensic heroes

Some scientists have spent their lives helping to solve hundreds of crimes...

Mathieu Orfila (1787-1853) solved many murders by identifying traces of poison in the bodies.

Alexandre Lacassagne (1843-1924) was the first to find clues in blood patterns, as well as in bullet striations.

Spanish doctor Mathieu Orfila develops the first tests that can find traces of blood at a crime scene.

Scottish chemist James Marsh uses a test to identify arsenic, and proves in court that a man was murdered by this deadly poison.

French doctor Bergeret d'Arbois pioneers forensic entomology by proving that a body covered in insects had been dead for many months.

French detective Alphonse Bertillon invents the system of recording photographs and noting down the physical details of all arrested suspects.

Austrian magistrate Hans Gross writes a book explaining how to gather evidence at a crime scene.

Argentinian detective Juan Vucetich becomes the first policeman to arrest a suspect based on fingerprint evidence.

French professor Alexandre Lacassagne first notices that bullets have unique markings on them caused by rifling in a gun barrel.

German serologist Max Richter develops a simple test to show which blood type a bloodstain belongs to.

German geologist Georg Popp solves a murder by analyzing traces of minerals found on a handkerchief.

French doctor Victor Balthazard is the first to analyze striations and firing-pin marks accurately.

French detective Edmund Locard sets up the world's first crime lab at the University of Lyon, France.

American medical student John Larson designs the first polygraph machine.

American investigator Luke May solves a kidnapping by examining matching knife marks under a microscope.

Scottish pathologist John Glaister records the differences between many kinds of human and animal hair.

American sleuth Frances Glessner Lee helps solve a number of crimes by reconstructing crime scenes using miniature models.

Swiss criminalist Max Frei-Sulzer invents the 'lifting' method of collecting small clues from crime scenes.

American psychologist James Brussel helps catch the 'mad bomber' who had been terrorizing New York by drawing up an accurate personality profile.

Canadian chemist Doug Lucas uses gas chromatography to identify different types of accelerant.

Japanese fingerprint examiners Matsumur and Soba develop the use of superglue to detect latent prints.

British engineers Foster and Freeman build the first Electro-Static detection Apparatus (ESDA).

British scientist Alec Jeffreys develops the first method for creating a DNA profile.

American doctor John Coe discovers that the amount of potassium in a dead person's eyes increases at a steady rate.

In Britain, the world's first DNA database is opened, collecting DNA profiles from all convicted criminals.

Hans Gross (1847-1915), often called the father of criminalistics, invented the crime scene evidence kit, and wrote the first book on forensics.

John Glaister (1892-1971) was the first doctor to show how to examine a corpse to determine the time of death.

Henry Lee (1938-) is a Chinese American scientist who has appeared as an expert witness at over 1,000 trials.

# Glossary

In this book there are many words that are often used when talking about crime, detection and court cases. Here, you can find out what they mean.

**accelerant** Any chemical that can start fires and explosions quickly.

**appeal** A *trial* that challenges an old *verdict*, often using new evidence.

**ballistics** The study of how bullets fly, also used to describe gun analysis.

**criminal investigation** Examining evidence to try to solve a crime.

**database** A long list, often on a computer, that holds information.

**decomposed** When a corpse is eaten away by insects until only the bones are left.

**diatoms** Creatures that live in water and can only be seen under a microscope.

**DNA** The complex chemical that makes each person unique.

**evidence** Anything that relates to a crime that can be used to help with an *investigation* or *trial*.

**firearms** Weapons that shoot objects at high speeds, such as guns.

**flammable** Anything that can catch fire easily.

**fragmentary evidence** Broken pieces from a crime scene that can be linked to pieces found on a suspect.

**latent** Describes evidence that is hard to find; often exposed using chemical sprays or special lights.

**polygraph** A machine that measures a person's reactions; sometimes known as a lie-detector.

**profile** A report on a person that describes different characteristics, such as their DNA or their personality.

**propellant** Any chemical that is used to fire a bullet from a gun.

**residue** Traces of chemicals.

**rifling** The grooves in a gun barrel.

**sentence** Punishment given to a person found guilty after a *trial*.

**striations** Marks on a used bullet.

**swab** Item used to collect liquid evidence from crime scenes and suspects.

**trace evidence** Very small clues.

**trial** When a person comes before a judge in a courtroom.

**verdict** The outcome of a *trial*, as decided by a judge or jury.

# Checklist of forensic scientists

**ballistics expert** Examines evidence left behind by bullets and guns.

**chemist** Studies traces of chemicals, such as suspicious gases found at the scene of a fire or explosion.

**psychologist** Studies the mind and creates personality profiles.

**dendrochronologist** Finds clues hidden in things made of wood.

**document examiner** Anlayzes clues from handwriting, ink and paper.

**entomologist** Studies insects.

**odontologist** Finds clues from teeth and bite marks.

**palynologist** Studies pollen left by plants and trees.

**pathologist** Doctor who performs autopsies and finds clues from dead bodies.

**serologist** Analyzes blood and DNA

**toxicologist** Looks for and analyzes traces of poisons.

# Checklist of crimes

There are many different types of crimes that people commit. Here, you can find out what they mean. In law books there are much more detailed definitions of each type of crime.

**arson** Starting a fire on purpose, in order to cause damage.

**blackmail** Demanding money from someone by threatening to reveal a secret about them to the public.

**burglary** Entering a building without premission and *stealing* something.

**forgery** Producing fake things such as artworks or money or signatures.

**fraud** Telling lies to help steal money.

**kidnapping** Taking a person and hiding them, then demanding money for their safe return.

**manslaughter** Killing a person by accident or to protect yourself.

**murder** Killing a person deliberately, also called homicide.

**robbery** Using violence to help *steal*.

**stealing** Taking something that belongs to someone else, also known as theft.

**terrorism** Killing people or blowing things up to make people afraid, often for a political reason.

# Internet links

There are lots of websites with information about forensic science, and activities to do using forensic science techniques. At the Usborne Quicklinks Website you'll find links to some great sites where you can:

- solve a crime using DNA evidence

- find out how to identify your own fingerprints

- read about real life criminals and how forensic scientists

  helped to capture them

- explore a crime scene to look for clues

- see pictures of bullets being compared under a microscope

- watch a video about forensic entomology

**For links to these sites and more, go to the Usborne Quicklinks Website at www.usborne-quicklinks.com and enter the keywords: forensic science.**

When using the Internet, please follow the Internet safety guidelines shown on the Usborne Quicklinks Website. The links at Usborne Quicklinks are regularly reviewed and updated, but Usborne Publishing is not responsible and does not accept liability for the content on any website other than its own. We recommend that children are supervised while using the Internet.

# Index

accelerant, 69, 73, 92
arson, 69, 93

ballistics, 60-67, 93
blood spatter, 21, 22, 24-25, 26, 65
blood, 8, 11, 12, 16, 21-27, 30, 33, 37, 40, 41, 58, 90
body, 11, 36-43, 45, 50, 51, 59, 85
bomb, 46, 68, 71-73, 74
bones, 33, 59
bullet case, 61, 62, 64
bullets, 8, 24, 40, 41, 60-67, 90
burglary, 16, 19, 25, 32, 93

camera, 11, 80, 83
cells, 29
computer, 11, 15, 16, 75, 77, 79-80
coroner, 5, 39
crime lab, 6, 10, 13, 33, 34, 53, 91, 92
Crime Scene Investigator (CSI), 4, 8, 10, 33, 45, 46, 47, 53, 54, 56, 63, 64
crime scene, 6, 10-11, 15, 25, 27, 32, 33, 53, 64-65, 66, 70, 85, 91

database, 20, 35, 43, 57, 92
defendant, 5, 12
DNA, 27, 28-35, 43, 46, 92
document examiner, 77-79, 93
dogs, 46, 70

Electro-Static Detection Apparatus (ESDA), 78-79, 91

entomologist, 44-45, 46, 93
expert witness, 5, 12-13, 91

fingerprint officer, 15, 16
fingerprints, 11, 14-20, 33, 43, 90
fire, 11, 41, 68-70, 71, 72
firearms, 60-61, 92
forensic accounting, 76-77
forgery, 75, 76, 77, 93
fragments, 49, 54, 72, 92
fraud, 77, 78, 80, 93

genes, 29
glass, 11, 53, 54
guns, 11, 61-67, 90

hairs, 7, 8, 51, 54, 91

identity, 20, 77, 78, 79, 82-85
insects, 11, 44-46, 90, 93
interrogation, 74, 86

judge, 5, 12-13, 29, 34
jury, 5, 29, 34, 67, 82

kidnapping, 50, 93

latent, 16-17, 26, 92
lawyer, 5, 12-13, 29, 39, 67

magnifying glass, 53
manslaughter, 66-67, 93

microscope, 53, 54, 55, 78, 91
modus operandi, 84-85
murder, 8, 9, 23, 35, 38, 42, 48, 55, 58, 85, 87, 93

pathologist, 37, 39, 93
poison, 40, 41, 42, 73, 90
pollen, 47, 48, 93
polygraph, 86, 91, 92
propellant, 61, 63, 92
psychologist, 84-85, 87, 89, 91, 93

rifling, 61, 62, 90, 91
robbery, 79, 88-89, 93

saliva, 11, 32
serologist, 22, 25, 27, 28, 31, 93
shoes, 7, 26, 27, 47, 56, 57
signature, 77
stealing, 25, 81, 83, 93
striation, 25, 81, 83, 93
swab, 63, 73, 92

teeth, 9, 43, 56, 57, 94
terrorism, 68, 74, 93
time of death, 36-37, 91
trace evidence, 7, 53, 54, 55, 90, 92
trial, 5, 7, 12-13, 93

voice prints, 84

wood, 49, 69

# Acknowledgements

Additional consultancy: Mike Gorn, LGC Forensics; Mike Allen, Document Evidence.
Source material for true crime stories taken from the following books:
*Written in Blood* by Colin and Damon Wilson, Constable & Robinson Ltd. 2003;
*The Casebook of Forensic Detection* by Colin Evans, John Riley & Sons 1996.
Digital imaging: Nick Wakeford. Gallery artwork on p25 and p27: Jonathan Chen,
Kimberley Chen and Natalie Chen.
Additional editorial material: Anna Claybourne, Louie Stowell

## Photo Credits

Key: (bd) background; (t) top; (b) bottom; (m) middle; (l) left; (r) right

Cover (bd) Mehau Kulyk / Science Photo Library (SPL); p6 Tek image / SPL; p8 Tek image / SPL;
p9 Andrew Lambert Photography / SPL; p15 (tr) © Bettmann / Corbis, (b) Stephen Moncrieff; p22
(b) Ed Reschke, Peter Arnold Inc. / SPL; p23 © PhotoSpin, Inc / Alamy; p26 courtesy of Mike Gorn,
LGC Forensics; p28 CNRI / SPL; p33 Michael Donne / SPL; p34 (t) Stephen Moncrieff, equipment
courtesy of Julian Bartrup, University of Lincoln Dept. of Forensic and Biomedical Science; (bl) CBS
Photo / Robert Voets Copyright 2005 CBS Broadcasting, Inc. and Alliance Atlantis, Inc. All Rights
Reserved. Taken from the comic CSI: Secret Identity, published by www.idwpublishing.com; p35 James
King-Holmes / SPL; p36 Gusto / SPL; p37 (r) Graeme Montgomery / Getty Images, (br) © Hemera
Technologies / Alamy; p39 (b) © Julie Plasencia / San Francisco Chronicle / Corbis; p40 (tl) ©
Royalty-Free / Corbis; p41 (tr) Biophoto Associates / SPL, (br) © Hemera Technologies / Alamy;
p42 Martin Dohrn / SPL; p43 (b) EMPICS / PA; p44 Dr. Keith Wheeler / SPL; p45 (bl and bm) Eye
of Science / SPL, (br) Volker Steger / SPL; p46 Mauro Fermariello / SPL; p47 (m) © SuperStock /
Alamy; p48 David Scharf / SPL; p49 © graficart.net / Alamy; p54 (tl) © Mikael Karlsson / Alamy,
(mlx2) Eye of Science / SPL, (bl) Andrew Syred / SPL; p55 © Mikael Karlsson / Alamy; p56 (b) ©
Pedro Luz Cunha / Alamy; p57 courtesy of Foster & Freeman; p63 © Getty Images; p68 © epa /
Corbis; p69 © sciencephotos / Alamy; p71 (br) Nicholas Veasey / Getty Images; p72 © Reuters /
Corbis; p74 Charles D. Winters / SPL; p75 courtesy of Foster & Freeman; p76 © Dennis Galante /
Corbis; p77 © Bettmann / Corbis; p78 (l) courtesy of Foster & Freeman; p79 (tl and r) courtesy of
Foster & Freeman; p82 © Image Source / Alamy; p86 (tl) Tek image / SPL; p87 SPL

First published in 2007 by Usborne Publishing Ltd. 83-85 Saffron Hill, London EC1N 8RT.

www.usborne.com